HORSE TALES

Teddy and Just'n
come to an
understanding

Horse Tales

ISBN: 978-0-9981719-3-7

Printed in the United States of America

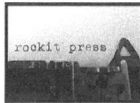

ROCKIT PRESS

ACKOWLEDGEMENTS

I would like to acknowledge my appreciation for Kim McElroy's beautiful poem, and for both my son, Johnny Daly, and my neighbor, Sammy Beining, for allowing their photos to be used.

Thanks as well to Shauna Jackson and Kate Crosby for their assistance in editing.

Thanks also to Locke Motley, my granddaughter, who served as our trusted junior editor and who proudly continues our family tradition of horse shows and winning.

Finally, the utmost appreciation goes to my husband, Steele Lipe, for integrating the photographs into the text and for his unwavering encouragement and support.

The content of this book is based on fact. However, to some extent, Teddy's tale is fictionalized although it is based on the author's personal experience, riding in horse shows, raising and racing thoroughbreds, participating in a few hunts, and now rescuing thoroughbred horses. The Ozzie tale is a true experience witnessed in Connecticut by the author. The Pegasus painting was also done by the author after a dream she had about Pegasus in the library. Enjoy all of the symbolism there!

"A good man will take care of his horses … not only while they are young, but when they are old and past service."

~ Plutarch

"Whenever an animal is somehow forced into the service of men, every one of us must be concerned for any suffering it bears on that account. No one of us may permit any preventable pain to be inflicted, even though the responsibility is not ours. No one may appease his conscience by thinking he would be interfering in something that does not concern him. No one may shut his eyes and think the pain, which is therefore not visible to him, is non-existent."

~ Albert Schweitzer

"God made the horse from the breath of the wind, the beauty of the earth, and the soul of an angel." (Author Unknown)

I AM

A ~ An Adaptable Ancestral Animal that can seem Aloof

B ~ I am Beloved because I am Benevolent, Beautiful, and Bold

C ~ I am Conscious therefore I am also Clairvoyant, Contradictory, and Cautious

D ~ I may seem Domesticated, but if you see me as Divine I express Depth and Devotion

E ~ I am Elemental, Emotional, Expressive, Empathetic, Enigmatic, Elegant, and Eloquent

F ~ I can be Formidable and Fearful but given Freedom I will be your Friend Forever

G ~ My spirit is Glorious, and I am full of Generosity

I am HORSE

Kim McElroy, artist, and poet, *'Spirit of the Horse.'*

Thoroughbreds are a breed of horses. They are best known for their agility and speed, especially running at the racetrack. They are very intelligent and, it is important to note, they are also sensitive.

Two thoroughbred horses, Teddy and Just'n, were roaming around the pasture, their heads down, noses even touching the ground. The Bahia grass they nibbled in the lush green grass field tasted so good, they could not resist. Their barn was nice, and their stalls were light and airy, but the sun was out and the grass and the breeze beckoned. Why stay inside? The Lady gave them free access to the pastures from their stalls, so out they went. After consuming enough grass, the two horses decided to get out of the sun and wandered over to the big tree in the far corner of their pasture. As they stood together, cooler under the shade of the old oak, Teddy decided it was a good time to talk. Since he had only recently arrived at this farm, he wanted to understand his new friend. And this is where their conversation began.

Teddy turned to Just'n and said, "It's so nice to be here and I like you; I really do. But why are you so bossy?" Just'n raised his head and looked directly at Teddy. His ears flipped with suspicion, as he considered the bluntness of his new friend's question.

"Because, for once, I can make my own decisions!" Just'n answered facing Teddy.

But Teddy was confused. "What do you mean?" Teddy asked as he flicked his tail to bat a fly.

Just'n snorted, then turned to check on another fly which landed on his rear. The fly was gone, so he faced Teddy and replied, "For years, I had to obey."

"Obey whom?" Teddy wanted to know. "Whom?" he asked again as he nudged Just'n on his side.

"The trainers!" Just'n proceeded to huff and snort and was about to walk away from this conversation.

"What are 'trainers'?" Teddy asked looking around as if "trainers" were possibly hiding in the pasture.

Surprised at such a question, Just'n stopped and turned around. "I was at the race tracks." He then proceeded to push his nose against Teddy's neck.

Teddy responded to the rub by raising his head and, looking directly into Just'n's eyes, asks, "Racetracks?"

"Yes, I was there to run, run fast, beat other horses. The riders are called Jockeys, and when they ride you in a real race, they wear fancy bright colored shirts and helmets. I would be washed and groomed and then walked to a saddling circle where I would meet with the trainer and get properly attired with a small saddle and a bridle. Then the jockey gets on. There is lots of noise coming from the crowds of people watching as you are paraded out to the track. You get to trot a little to warm up; then you are ridden into one of the many stalls in a long starting gate. But you need to focus, and the focus is on speed. So when the gates open and the race begins, I do what we have rehearsed; I run. I give what the jockey wants: speed." Now Just'n is bored with this conversation and wants to go back to grazing.

But Teddy persists and pursues. "Why? I mean why did you have to go to the track and run?"

Just'n snorts, kicks away another fly but knows he needs to answer Teddy's question. "To make money for my owners by winning." Grazing would have to wait.

"I do not understand." Teddy turns toward Just'n almost pleading for an explanation.

"I am famous. I was born in Kentucky. My ancestors were famous. *Bold Ruler* for one." Just'n is sure Teddy will understand and expects great respect once he knows this. Instead, Teddy replies, "*Bold Ruler*? Who is he?"

Just'n decides to ignore Teddy's ignorance, so he continues. "Yes, famous, many famous racehorses. *Nashua, Northern Dancer*...."

Teddy interrupts because this does not make sense to him. "But...."

Just'n continues so Teddy might understand. "They expected me to run like these other horses that I am related to. But I couldn't. I tried! However, I only won a few times." That is enough talking, he decides, as he wanders back into the field and begins to graze.

But Teddy follows him and wants to know more. "How long did you have to do that job?"

Just'n raises his head, looks toward the barn, then back at Teddy. "Six years."

Teddy's eyes open wide as he considers what Just'n just said. "Wow, six years! That is a long time."

Just'n had begun to nibble the grass again, but he stopped and looked up. Teddy was staring at Just'n's neck."What's that strap around your neck?" Teddy asked.

Just'n replied, "It is called a cribbing strap. Cribbing is a bad habit that I have and it is hard to break. When I was at the race track, I got bored standing in my stall with nothing to do until it was my turn to run. I would be stuck inside for hours and hours waiting for the next chance to get out, have the jockey put a bit in my mouth, saddle on my back, and hop on. Then off we would go, running on the track. That part I enjoyed. Running. Yes, running as fast as I could. Sometimes it was in the morning, and often we were the only ones on the track. But sometimes, it was in the afternoon. That was when, after a brief warm-up, I had to enter the starting gate in a stall side by side with other horses.

When it was afternoon racing time, I couldn't concentrate since there were crowds of people in the grandstand yelling. But once the bell went off and the gates opened, I was out and running. I had to try and beat the other horses to the finish line. My jockey would guide me, but often I was stuck behind or in the middle of the pack and couldn't get to the front." Just'n paused. Then he added, "So I lost."

Teddy stared at Just'n, his eyes wide open. All this was new information for him.

Just'n sighs, then continues his tale. "But when I didn't get to run, I spent hours alone in the stall. I was bored. Teddy, you have seen me grab hold of things like the stall door or the side of the bucket or a fence post. I use my upper teeth to grab something and suck in air, and it gives me a good feeling. I think the feel-good chemicals are from my nervous system. They are called endorphins. They calm me and relieve some of the stress I used to feel. Anyway, the humans call it 'cribbing.' I don't do it as much anymore since I am so much happier, but The Lady put this strap around my neck to be sure that when I do crib, I don't take in too much air because it comes in and goes down into my stomach. Too much air could make me sick. But now, it is no longer stress; it is a habit. And yes, I know, a *baaaad* habit. But I can't quit!" Just'n sighs, clears his throat and considers returning to nibbling grass. But then he pauses and decides to explain a bit more. "Back to the race track," he begins. Teddy moves closer, not to miss a word. "Those years racing, I was in California. Then the owners brought me East, to a racetrack in Maryland."

"What happened?" Teddy asks, his eyes open wide in anticipation of what he assumed would be something positive, perhaps exciting.

"I got hurt," Just'n replied as he turned away from Teddy and looked for more grass to munch.

Teddy was astonished. "Oh my! What…."

Before Teddy could finish, Just'n's head rose up from the grass. Now facing Teddy, he replied, "I have a bone chip. It is like a broken bone that

didn't heal. It is in my right front leg. I couldn't race anymore because it hurt to run."

Teddy was shocked. He stamped his feet, pawed the ground, and then decided to ask: "Did a veterinarian treat you? I know what a vet is; at least, thanks to the nice Lady, I now know. He is that man who came to the barn a few weeks ago. He worked on my leg and made me feel better when I was cut after getting too close to that broken fence post." Teddy paused, looked down at his leg, gave his healed cut a lick, then asked, "So, Just'n, did you see a vet?"

Just'n's ears went flat, and he wrinkled his nose. Then, after a pause, he neighed his answer: "Nnnooooo."

Teddy was amazed. "Why not?" he asked.

"It would cost the owner money. So he put me up for sale; put me in an auction." Not wanting to remember this part of his past, Just'n left Teddy's side and walked off to graze.

Nevertheless, Teddy followed him. "What is that?" He was perplexed. "What is an auction?"

Just'n tried to ignore the question. It was a sale. The buyers were not nice, and many of the horses were taken away, crammed into horse trailers with no room to turn and no food or water to drink. He had heard the word 'slaughter' used by the men dragging these sweet souls out of the building and into the trailers.

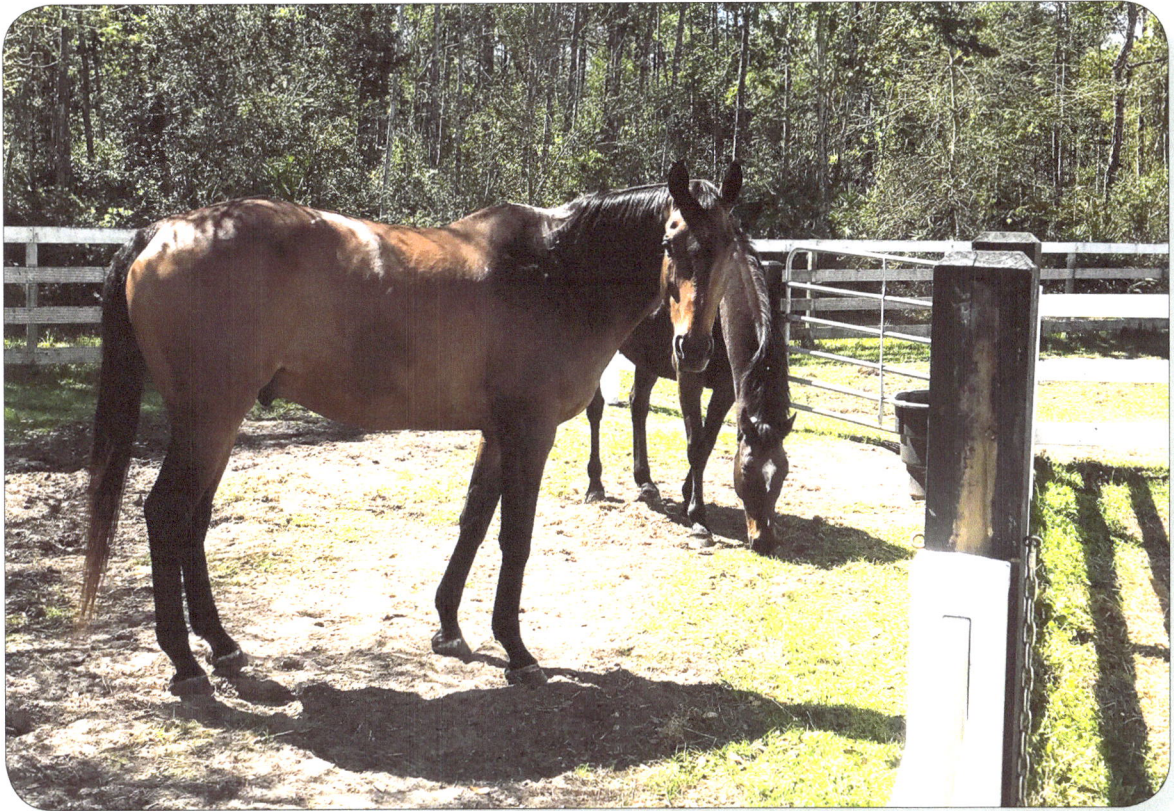

Fortunately, this was not to be his fate. Instead, he was purchased by a man who took him to his farm in West Virginia and — no, that is another story and not a tale to tell Teddy. Not this time.

Teddy came over and was standing by his side, but Just'n knew Teddy would not understand so he kept pulling up grass into his mouth. Finally, however, he decided he had to give some response. To make it short and end the conversation, he simply said, "You don't want to know."

For a while, side by side, in silence, the two horses continued grazing, pulling up the new grass, munching, drooling, enjoying the moment. Then Teddy could not help himself. He had to ask one more question.

"How did you get here?"

Ok, Just'n was going to finish this conversation on a positive note. "I got lucky," he replied looking back toward the house on the hill. There was good news worth sharing. And the good news was how this nice lady, the one who lives in that house overlooking the pasture, came into his life.

"This Lady takes care of me, loves me. She named me 'Just'n' because, she said, she found and bought me 'just in time.' It is from an old song's lyrics: 'Just in time, we found you just in time…' It is too late to fix my leg, but until last year, I let her ride me."

Teddy was amazed. "And now?"

To this question, Just'n was content to respond. His ears shot up, and he looked directly at Teddy. With a grin, he said, "Now I am happy to be with you!" Then he made his point by rubbing his head against Teddy's neck.

The two horses roamed around the field, searching for more tall grass to munch. Then they went to the water tub and took some sips. When Just'n finished drinking the water, he stood back and decided it was Teddy's turn.

"Teddy, you are a Thoroughbred too. But you didn't race. Tell me, what is your tale?"

"My tail?" Teddy replied swishing his tail in the breeze.

Just'n shook his head, "No, your story!"

"Oh, yes, my life before we met," Teddy replied twitching his nose. Flies were abuzz. But the conversation was not over. "I think I was supposed to race like you. But my owner died."

"Sad."

"Yes. Then I was sent to a man who tried to make me do whatever he wanted. But I didn't understand what it was that he wanted." Teddy hated to remember those days. But Just'n wanted to know. Teddy realized how difficult it was for Just'n to share his story, so he had to tell his own tale. That was only fair.

"So what happened?" Just'n repeated since Teddy had taken a long pause.

Teddy's ears went back. He clenched his teeth. Those times, his past, he just wanted to get rid of the memories. But he had to be honest, so he replied, "First he would put a bit in my mouth, but if I shook my head, he would slap me in the face with his hand. I shook my head because the bit was not soft. It had a rough edge that hurt my mouth. But after the bit, he put on a saddle and, to keep it in place, he tightened the girth real hard under my belly. That hurt. Then he climbed up and got on. But once he was settled in his saddle, he rode me to a ring. We began by walking around, then we trotted around, then we cantered around the ring. The ring had fences in it. So around we went. I was supposed to canter to these fences and jump. I like to jump over fences, so I thought this would be fun. However, the man would kick my sides going toward the jumps. He wouldn't let me decide my speed or where to take the leap I needed to make it over the jump. Instead, he hit me over and over flogging me behind while, at the same time, he tugged and pulled on the bit in my mouth. So did he want me to slow down or go faster? I couldn't tell."

"What was he using to hit you?" Just'n asked.

"When he hit me, it was something he held. I think it was a stick. So, as we approached a jump, his hand reached back and he used this stick to hit my sides."

Just'n nodded. "You mean a crop?"

Teddy replied with a sigh, "Yes, I guess that is what some call it. He seemed to want me to slow up as he pulled on the reins or speed up as he hit me with that crop. I didn't know what he wanted, but between the pulling on my mouth and hitting my side, it hurt! It really hurt!"

"What did you do?" Just'n asked.

"I tried to get away from him," Teddy replied, angry that he had to remember any of this.

Just'n persisted. "Did you? I mean, did you get away from the man?"

Teddy hated remembering, hated the memory of trying to get away from that man. But he had to finish telling his tale. "No. He had a hold of me. If I jerked away, if I turned to left or right so we could leave the ring, he got mad. His hands held the reins. When he pulled back on the reins, the bit in my mouth pulled against my teeth. The more I tried to get away, the more he pulled. When he pulled like that, my head was forced to go down so I couldn't move forward. I couldn't get away."

"That must have hurt," Just'n said.

"Yes, it did. … A lot. So finally I bucked! Off he went! Down into the dirt. But I didn't care anymore. I ran back to the barn without him!" Now Teddy was ready to walk away from this conversation. And he did, but just a few steps around the old oak tree and up the slope. Then he paused, turned toward Just'n, and decided to tell the rest of his tale. "Yes, after falling off when I bucked, the man decided to get rid of me."

Just'n was shocked that his new sweet, quiet friend had done anything mean like bucking. But Teddy proceeded to tell what happened next.

"After a few months just standing around at a stable with nothing to do since that man didn't want to ride me anymore, I ended up with another man. At first, he seemed nice. But his sport was different. He wanted to take me to what they call a hunt. For the hunt, someone takes you to a place where riders and horses gather together. After the Master makes the morning announcements, and introduces the field masters, the huntsman gives a very short toot to get the hounds' attention and then usually moves off briskly or at least "with purpose". So off they go, all together, and follow the hound dogs. These dogs run and bark. The other horses told me the hounds were looking for a fox. We horses and our riders followed up and down and around. At first. I thought this was fun. There were hedges to jump over and streams to run through and sometimes fences to jump over too."

"So you were happy?"

"In the beginning, yes. But after a while, running behind the hounds, I was having trouble keeping up with the other horses. Then all of a sudden, as we were crossing a road to get to another field, a truck approached. The horn honked. The truck was huge and the horn was loud. I was scared. I bolted. Then I reared because I didn't know if the truck was going to stop. The truck was right there and honking. When I reared up, my rider could not stay on and slid off. Yes, he fell onto the hard surface of the road. I did try stopping, but it was too late. My rider was off. I don't know how the other horses got away, but I stayed and stood by my rider. I felt bad. Slowly, he stood up. Then he yelled. At me! Not at the truck driver, but at me! I think the other riders just wanted to keep up with the hounds. Run, run, run! Chase after the hounds. So they kept going, leaving us behind. When my rider remounted, we were too far behind. We couldn't find the hunt. My rider was very angry. The next day he took me to another barn and I was put out in a field."

"Oh my, what a bad experience! But going to a field, was that nice?"

"Yes and no. No more running, but I was alone. No one to talk to and no one who cared. Just me and the birds and squirrels and, of course, insects!" With this said, Teddy wandered away, tasted some grass, then moved on.

Just'n followed him. When they reached the edge of the pasture, Just'n looked up at the house, turned to Teddy, and said, "But now you are here, and you let The Lady hug you."

Teddy halted, turned around and, facing Just'n, replied, "Yes, it took me awhile to be able to trust her." Teddy could not help but smile. "But

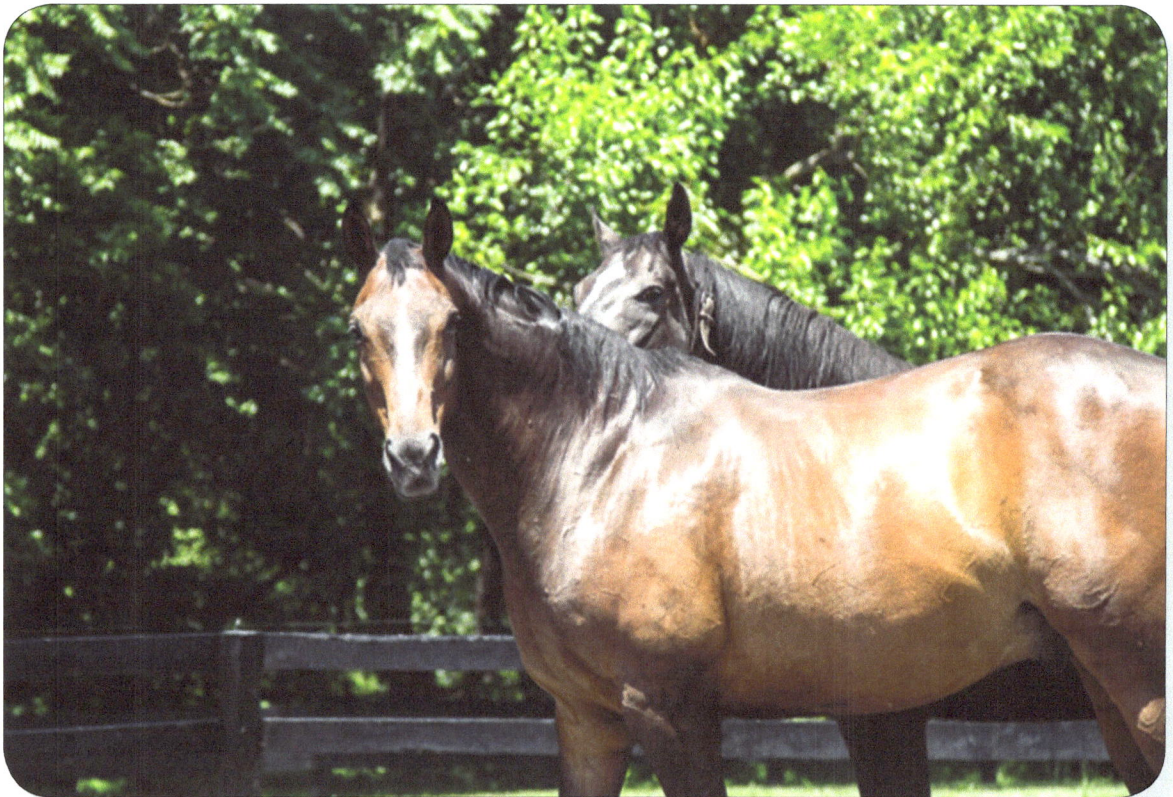

now I know a human CAN be nice!" Teddy was looking directly at The Lady's house.

Just'n followed his gaze, then asked, "How did you come here?"

Teddy wasn't sure. "I don't know," he said. "One day while I was out in that field, the field where I had been left, left for a long time, maybe months, but this one day, a man opened the gate and walked onto the field. I watched as he came over to me. I had been eating the grass, although there wasn't much. It was in Florida and hot. But there was a pond, so I drank a lot of water. The nights were nice. But on this day, this man walked directly to me. He patted me, and he spoke to me softly. He was very friendly. I felt comfortable with him and relaxed. Then he put a halter over my head and led me out of the field. But we weren't going for a ride. Instead, he took me into a trailer, a big trailer pulled by a truck. Although the man was nice, I was scared inside the trailer. I asked myself, was I going to be taken to another mean person, to somewhere awful? Maybe I would be killed. But no! That man driving the truck brought me here."

Just'n looked directed at Teddy. "You are happy now, aren't you?"

Teddy returned Just'n's stare and replied with a grin, "Yes, very happy. Now The Lady's son rides me from time to time, and we jump."

Just'n had never jumped so he had to ask, "Now you jump for fun? At least it looks like you are having fun."

"Yes," Teddy replied. "He rides me bareback, which I love, and over the fences, we go. He doesn't pull on the reins. He lets me find my spot to take off and jump. Great fun."

Just'n laughed. "I love watching you!" He paused and, looking directly at Teddy, added, "I'm so glad you are here now!"

Teddy smiled. "And I love being here with you!"

"I also love when children come here to visit us," Teddy continued. "I hear that some kids can relate to us better than they can relate to other humans."

"Yes." Just'n agreed. "We horses understand what the child's heart is saying. We can feel emotions and respond. It is called compassion. It is a feeling many people, especially adults, often cannot understand."

Speaking about children, Teddy butted in. "I have another tale to tell. I remember one time a little boy was asked to pat me. It was when I was alone in that big field. I was so happy to see a child. I could speak with him, I thought. But I noticed the boy was scared. Maybe it was because I was so big. So I didn't run up to him. Instead, since he was frightened, I decided not to run and jump with glee even though that was what I felt like doing. Instead, I slowly walked over to him. But when I came close, he still seemed frightened. So, slowly, I came up beside him, then stood still. I put my head down. I even had my nose next to his cheek. And I waited. The boy began to move away. But then I noticed a lady had come with the boy, and she said, 'Pat him. Pat the sweet horse.' And the boy did. His pat was nice and soft. I did not move. It felt good. I knew the boy was no longer scared of me. The next time the boy came to my field, I knew, and he knew, we were friends. No fear. Sadly, I only saw him two more times before I left that field. But now, of course, I am here with you! And now, I have lots of friends!"

Just'n shook his head and whinnied. He liked this story.

The two horses decided to leave the shade of the old oak tree and stroll back out into the sun to graze. But Just'n suddenly stopped. He remembered another story from his past, a tale told to him by another horse, a horse named Ozzie. They had met at a stable where Just'n trained before he went to the racetrack.

"Teddy, I have one more tale to tell you. It is about a horse named Ozzie. He told me he used to be ridden by children, children with what he called 'disabilities.' It was, he said, a small group of equestrian women who had begun a program for children, a program of healing by riding. They brought in horses like Ozzie for these children to ride. They called the program *Pegasus*, named for a winged horse from Greek mythology. They said Pegasus was a model for inspiration and hope for these kids."

"Getting back to your tale, what was wrong with the children?" Teddy asked.

"I think they had either a problem with moving or a problem speaking. Ozzie told me about one little boy who was placed on him. After the boy was in the saddle on his back, one person stood on one side of Ozzie and another person stood on the other side. Then the walker came to lead Ozzie forward. But before they started the walk, all the people would say, 'walk on' and the name of the horse the child was riding. On this one day, before the people could say, 'Walk on, Ozzie,' the little boy began to speak. Slowly, he said: 'Waaaaalk ooonnn Ozzzzi.' Everyone had tears in their eyes. Ozzie wondered why they were all about to cry. Then the lady leading him for the walk told the others that this was the first time she had heard the boy speak! He had not said a word in four years!"

Teddy grinned. "Great story," he said waving his tail. Yes, Teddy understood.

Before going back to munching grass, Just'n added, "Ozzie was happy to help. Being with kids is always a happy event for us horses."

Like children, all horses deserve to be loved and treated kindly. These two "boys" are loved by everyone who meets them, especially a little girl named Sammy who comes to visit the boys and treats them with carrots or apples. When Sammy and other children are with a horse, they are not focused on themselves. They forget their troubles and just as Sammy said, they "want to ride and feel free." It is love both ways. Once you have the trust of a horse, you have a friend for life.

And as for Just'n and Teddy? These two horses will continue to grow old together, telling each other tales in a big field with a nice barn and a lady who, along with her family and friends, loves them.

www.ingramcontent.com/pod-product-compliance
Lightning Source LLC
LaVergne TN
LVHW072101070426
835508LV00002B/203